Paint to Remember

Stories of Soul Memories

Katherine J. Keilman

Copyright © 2012 Katherine J. Keilman

Cover Illustrations by Katherine J. Keilman

All rights reserved. No part of this book may be used or reproduced by any means, graphic, electronic, or mechanical, including photocopying, recording, taping or by any information storage retrieval system without the written permission of the publisher except in the case of brief quotations embodied in critical articles and reviews.

ISBN: 978-1-4525-4923-1 (sc)
ISBN: 978-1-4525-4922-4 (e)

Library of Congress Control Number: 2012905421

Balboa Press books may be ordered through booksellers or by contacting:

Balboa Press
A Division of Hay House
1663 Liberty Drive
Bloomington, IN 47403
www.balboapress.com
1-(877) 407-4847

Because of the dynamic nature of the Internet, any web addresses or links contained in this book may have changed since publication and may no longer be valid. The views expressed in this work are solely those of the author and do not necessarily reflect the views of the publisher, and the publisher hereby disclaims any responsibility for them.

The author of this book does not dispense medical advice or prescribe the use of any technique as a form of treatment for physical, emotional, or medical problems without the advice of a physician, either directly or indirectly. The intent of the author is only to offer information of a general nature to help you in your quest for emotional and spiritual well-being. In the event you use any of the information in this book for yourself, which is your constitutional right, the author and the publisher assume no responsibility for your actions.

Any people depicted in stock imagery provided by Thinkstock are models, and such images are being used for illustrative purposes only.
Certain stock imagery © Thinkstock.

Printed in the United States of America

Balboa Press rev. date:4/2/2012

Paint to Remember
Stories of Soul Memories

"Bringing memories of other times and places into your current reality unifies the significance of your life."
—*The Pleiadians*

Dedicated to

Kristine, Patricia, Michael, Marie and Jason

Contents

Introduction	xiii
Chapter 1: Paint to Remember	1
Chapter 2: Cabin in the Woods	12
Chapter 3: Cliff Jumper	19
Chapter 4: Reconnecting with My Healing Tools	25
Chapter 5: Missing the Boat	30
Chapter 6: Victorian Pansies	33
Chapter 7: The Wizard	38
Chapter 8: Final Comments	41
Rainbow Rain Meditation	43
My Favorite Books	45
About the Author	47

Introduction

The following pages contain short stories that relate to my journey with teachers and mentors who have had other lifetimes with me. I met them again in this lifetime to resolve some issue from our past. In each chapter you will find a combination of memoir, fiction, and writings from my journal notes that represent some personal healing gained through remembering a past lifetime. The fiction describes the potential for a new experience that could unfold, filling the space cleared by the healing. Each of these fictional new experiences can represent hidden desires and dreams that bring immense joy into a person's life. For me, some of that "fiction" is being realized.

Past life work has had an incredible effect upon my life. In a subtle way, I had believed that other lifetimes were something that other people experienced. At first, I avoided it, saw no reason to go there, and considered it a waste of time. When I finally did get curious, I spent almost three years trying to find out everything I could about every one of my past lives. I eventually grew tired of spending so much time in it, and now I use it only to help clear any issue that seems difficult to resolve. While the past life work can have great results, it is not to be taken lightly.

Understanding the information brought forth by the past life work was not easy. The words I wrote in journals often appeared somewhat incoherent and disjointed. For a long time, the notes seemed like puzzle pieces that did not match anything. Within a year, I had filled two large journals with messages. Some information was relevant to the time it was written, but there were other pages that did not seem to go with any of the events in my life. Those pieces eventually started revealing themselves as unresolved issues from other lifetimes.

The biggest revelation was the concept that my soul chose everything for the learning experience, ultimately leading back to unconditional love. You might have heard someone comment about some tragedy by saying, "Why did that have to happen?" This kind of question places blame on others. When I want to better understand some personal event, I ask "What has my soul designed for me to learn from this experience?" This is my way of taking responsibility.

As I recognized that my soul chose the experiences for this lifetime, I began to better understand the bumps in my path. I began remembering that I was a member of a soul group that had agreed to help others achieve their chosen assignments. Our experiences include what appear to be both positive and negative events. We start our human existence with no memory of those choices, as if we were leaving the script behind. Many of us begin our lives experiencing our challenging events (negative) more strongly than the fun, encouraging events (positive), and it can take us a long time to recognize our life's mission. Since we did all the choosing, then the effects of our experiences are neither negative nor positive --- just perfect in their unfolding.

Through intense personal and spiritual work, I began to understand that some of my chaos, crises, strong emotions, etc., were associated with other lifetimes, and some issues had even been handed down from ancestors. Clearing these obstacles through past life regression and meditation created new space in this lifetime that has allowed me to do things that I truly enjoy. In the process, I am joyfully completing my soul's choices. If you are considering this kind of work, I recommend that you take the time to find the technique and the practitioner that resonates with you.

I have included a list of my favorite books, the ones that have been most helpful during my personal journey. When recommending books, I let people know what I have used and suggest they start with smaller/thinner books because their information is often more to the point. I also suggest going to a bookstore to just stand in front of the shelves until your eyes or hands seem to unconsciously pick something. I have not included books about past lives because I did not find those books appealing until after I had done much of my own personal work.

When it comes to journaling, I recommend that you write as if you will never read the words again. This helps the flow, and it can act as an emotional release. It's also a good idea to carry a small journal with you or in the car for quick notes.

Best wishes for your own journey. Enjoy.

Katherine Keilman
2012

Paint to Remember

My Potential Future

I stopped my car in front of my studio. Before going in to meet the crowd that was waiting for me, I reminisced about the beginning of this adventure. After a deep breath and taking the time to get centered, I was grateful that I had finally listened to the words my spirit guides had repeated to me on several occasions: *paint to remember*.

This particular journey began in 2000 with a move to Houston, Texas. Life had not been particularly fun for a long time, and a corporate invitation had given me the opportunity to start fresh without any close family members looking over my shoulder. Many of those family members were difficult to be around, and I only recognized the rampant codependency after moving. The blessing in disguise was the 1,100-mile distance that opened a space for me to rediscover an empathetic and intuitive nature that had been silenced in early childhood.

Within a year of my move, I was working with different intuitives and healing practitioners. A year later, I went to massage therapy school, received Reiki attunements, and began a deeper exploration of the energy pathways of the body. For the last several years, I have been journaling conversations with my angels and spirit guides. There were many stories of other lifetimes; some describing the healing techniques that I had been using in my own practice in this lifetime.

When I moved to Springfield, Missouri, I easily connected with people in the metaphysical and spiritual communities. The city felt very much like my hometown. Some form of autopilot switched on because, within days of moving into my apartment, I began new efforts with personal, physical, and spiritual healing. These included eating locally grown organic foods, receiving energy work, and getting regular massages, acupuncture, and spinal adjustments. I began devoting most of my time to writing a book based on some journal notes about other lifetimes. Within six months, the book had been sent to a publisher and was on store shelves before my next birthday. Then I switched to spending most of my time painting.

Now I was getting ready to enjoy the results of those efforts. My studio was located in the older part of town. The whole block of buildings had been preserved by historical organizations. The first time I walked through the two-story section, I felt an unusual kinship with the rooms, as if I were coming home. I converted the front side of the building into an art studio. The back of the building held a large comfortable office that I used for my writing studio. It opened out to a small garden that was shaded by a couple of mature native oak trees.

As I walked up to the front of the building, the antique glass door opened to reveal a crowded room of friends and patrons in quiet conversation about the artwork. I had been selling my paintings for two years, but my intention for opening this gallery was to create a space for other intuitive artists.

That day's event was devoted to my work and introductions of future shows with other artists. In the days before the show, a couple of close friends helped hang each painting in just the right spot. As they went on the wall, I felt the glow of unconditional love flowing through each canvas. I felt successful knowing that every time I prepared to paint, I had asked for guidance to instill the energy of its new owner in the work. I watched visitors stop to absorb each painting before moving to the next. A few people stopped in their tracks in front of one work in particular and did not move for several minutes. I smiled because I knew they would become the new owners of that piece of artwork. I walked around the room, answering questions and saying hello to everyone. After stepping away from the last group, I scanned the room and watched as sold tags were placed on a number of the paintings. People were not wasting any time making sure they took home the ones they liked. I closed my eyes to visualize how each of the new owners seemed to tune into his or her painting, standing in front of it for the first time, sensing it had been painted just for him or her.

Turning to move toward a new group of visitors, I came face-to-face with a former teacher and mentor. Memories flashed before me. I had worked with him for a number of years. First, I was a client, then an employee, and finally, a student as he helped me develop a certain area of my intuitive skills. I had been a new massage therapist when I started seeing forgotten trauma in the body, and he had shown me how to help my clients release the emotions of old trauma from the physical body. He had been one of my favorite teachers, but things changed when I began noticing that he only wanted me around to help maintain a protective shield of energy in our work space. We went our separate ways when I finally recognized that he was not going to accept me as a peer. After some past life work, I knew that my lessons with him were complete.

Our conversation was interrupted by the laughter of a short, round man in the company of two very tall, attractive young ladies. He walked briskly toward me, arms opening wide for a hug. He was another one of my teachers. The young women were his granddaughters, and they seemed to float across the floor as they walked from one painting to the next. They were Star Children. (Star Children are very telepathically connected to a worldwide network of other Star Children with life missions of helping the earth and its people with major shifts toward a higher consciousness.) More memories flowed. I smiled at how much this man always knew about me, and how he always stopped short of telling me the next step of what he could teach me during our work together. One hard lesson he taught me was to not be so willing to give up my cash. I learned that just because I have it is no reason to give it away.

I looked around the room and watched my sister at work. About the time I started painting classes, our relationship did a 180-degree turn. We have kept in touch with each other ever since. She was there to keep an eye on the catering for the event. She loved being in charge of that type of thing. After I turned it all over to her, she had worked with the local vendors to handle all the food, drink, and decorations. I had to pull her back a little on her decorating ideas, but she had accepted my words the first time—that was so different from past experiences.

During most of her life, she had endured many challenges, some rather dramatic, and she was still in the midst of some intense choices about her future. She was surviving, and it was great to have her with me for the opening.

Journal Notes of a Relevant Other Lifetime

I had been sitting at my table for a journaling meditation when the vision of a different lifetime appeared. A female guide that I did not recognize invited me to walk up some stairs. The steps and the walls were made of large, gray stones, and I had the impression that they would be cold if I were able to touch them. We walked up three landings and then through a doorway that opened to a beautiful roof garden. In one direction, there were hundreds of miles of rolling hills and green fields. Several hundred yards in the opposite direction was a forest.

The guide reached her hand out to me again, pulling me to the edge of the garden. Looking out at all the lush greenery, she said, "This was all yours. It can be again." My tears fell as if I was being reunited with something precious. I didn't want to stop the vision; as I strengthened my hold on her hand, my midsection felt as if it had been brutally punched.

When I asked her about it, she told me that it had been caused by an injury from the lifetime that I was remembering. She told me that it was time for healing, time to forgive everyone's part in that event. A flood of memories began to flow, showing me how it all had been taken away from me; I had been forced to live away from my family, the rooms, and the people I had grown up with.

She changed the subject for a moment and pointed to the small lapis beads around my neck. She explained that lapis was a good thing, and that it indicated royalty. She told me that it was time to take a rest, but I didn't want to, and tears fell once again.

Recognizing the view and the conversation with the new guide had made me weary. I stopped the meditation to nap. My stomach ached as if I had been breathing hard, and my breathing had become very shallow. Just before falling asleep, the stomach pain rose into my heart area in a sharp line, radiating from the center of my chest as if something sharp had struck me. The pains felt like the reference to that other lifetime. When I awakened, I was glad that my stomach no longer hurt. The time frame felt like the Mayan era, but the clothing did not seem to be correct.

Back in meditation, I saw my guide's face again. She was gleaming at my writing this. She had been waiting. She took my hand again, and we walked around the rooftop to look at the expanse of lands before us. She looked at me and whispered that this could be mine again—in this lifetime. I felt overwhelmed, but I sensed that what she said could be true. I embraced the hugeness of what it meant. I sighed and knew it was mine.

There was some resistance in me as she pulled me to another room. This was where the weariness originated. This was the room where my physical body had been killed in that lifetime. I saw my body on the floor in front of us, and my guide told me to pick up the headband that appeared to be made of gold and lapis. The room became brighter. The body on the floor faded away, and I felt more at ease for viewing this room in which I had slept. The walls were covered with layers of brocades in shades of gold and brown. The beautiful room was a little cluttered, but it was clean and airy.

I had been royalty in that lifetime, but I had not been treated in a royal fashion by my family. There were many others around me who treated me with a sense of very high regard. I was the Royal Seer. Many of my childhood teachers had quit because they had been afraid of the things I could see and predict. Two teachers stayed with me for many years, but as I grew older, I recognized how much they wished to manipulate me. I gradually spent less and less time with them.

During the next meditation, my guide and I walked up the stairs again. I felt a deep sense of anticipation. We were going to look around my room at the things that represented my work. We went to a large table on the side of the huge fireplace. A stack of journals contained a description of the healing work I had done with people and lengthy details of how people had been healed. The pages glowed as they were opened. (My left hand burns and pulses slightly as I write this, and it begins pulsing again as I type the words. I wonder if my computer is safe and go find my rose quartz bracelet).

I sensed my hands on the pages of those leather-bound journals and close my eyes to drink in the information. I could feel who I was in that lifetime and remembered the trips to the village. This guide had been my closest friend, and I wanted to see her and hear her say her name. I sensed that it was her eyes that I have doodled when I was bored at work; I had known those eyes belonged to someone who was watching over me. We had missed each other, but she was there to help awaken my healing powers. There was much work to be done, and she knew I was ready to begin. Focusing became difficult, and the word forgiveness came to mind. I felt a deep need to forgive the people in that lifetime. It had been carried into the present and was something that had been left unfinished.

I no longer had to meditate to sense my new guide. One day, she finally told me her name. Ceci was short for Cecilia. I could just about see her face. Only her blonde curly hair was clear to me, and I smiled as I remembered it causing her some trouble with the men. We had been inseparable since this remembering began; I felt her throughout my day.

I was on my way to work. She did not like my boss. The day before, she had explained that he connects to my energy and takes advantage of the loose hold I have on my space. For a moment, I thought about what part he might have played in the lifetime she had been helping me remember. I recognized this boss as my younger brother in the lifetime that Ceci had taken me to visit. He had orchestrated his placement into power after our father died even though I was older by several years. He was the royalty that I worked for, and he always kept me busy painting. I quietly said to myself that I had chosen not to be in service to him in this lifetime.

We returned to that other lifetime to reminisce about everyday life. I had a good life, dressed well in long layers of browns and golds. I stood in the middle of my room, slowly turning to take a look at the decorations. Heavy drapes or tapestries and several paintings covered the stone walls. A large painting on the wall near the fireplace showed a scene of trees and a distant river. I checked for a little dog in the room, but the one I saw was not little at all. The big one that I see shared Ruby's spirit.

Ruby, a rat terrier that I'd had since Christmas 2006, whined at me until I moved to the couch to write. She curled up in my lap as I continued writing. The big dog took notice. His questioning eyes gave me the impression that he wanted to do the same thing. In that lifetime, he often rested his head on my arm while I sat next to the fire.

During a break between meditations, I consulted with two intuitive friends. They told me that the healing techniques described in those journals have come back to me in this lifetime. They told me that I used my energy to loosen and pull illness out of a body. I directed energy into the space to speed the healing process. People were healed in miraculous ways, but I had to hide it and keep it a secret. They explained that Ceci was my contact to the outer community.

I was not married and did not have any children. With my healing work and being in service to my family, I did not have time for it. Because I was often weary after a session, my family soon realized that I was doing something with my time that did not involve them. This irritated some of them, and their renewed expectations called me into service at any time of the day or night.

Ceci and I were back in my room in that other lifetime. I sat in a comfortable, high-back chair with the dog's head on my arm. Oscar was a loose-skinned, lazy, long-eared hunting dog. With her hands, Ceci showed me how I used to do my work. Before me unfolded a scene with a villager being healed using a grid above his body. I saw myself pumping energy through the grid, fixing bumps and tears that were affecting the physical body. I also curled my fingertips as if to scoop out a sticky gray mess of illness, then filled the space with energy and sent more energy into the grid above the body. As I finished, small white flowers filled the edges of the grid, flowing as if they were a vine cascading from a trellis.

She told me that I rarely felt any pain while I was working on anyone. Villagers had nearly immediate results and were sent home to eat lightly, drink water, and rest for three days. Most of the time, it was very easy work. Occasionally there would be a growth that had stubborn tentacles branching into the surrounding tissue. That stubbornness was always related to the client's willingness to let go of the emotion or of their attachments to the illness. Healing occurs when it is desired—and when there is faith that it will occur.

I saw myself walking through a clearing of the forest that I had seen earlier. As I walked among the trees, I could see and feel the energies that radiated from them. The sun barely penetrated the branches of the huge trees. It felt like late afternoon. There was warmth in the radiant feeling in the forest's energies. Ceci told me that I always liked walking in the woods, adding that she was always watchful to keep the guards away while I refreshed my energies after a day of working with the villagers.

Henry, a helper in the village, was the contact that secretly made the arrangements for those who wanted healings. We often met them at the tailor's house. There were always people to turn away because there was not much time. (Henry is my dad in this lifetime. I recognized after he passed that he was in the current lifetime as my protector. The days before and after his passing, he appeared to me while I worked. He had such a soft and gentle look about him. He was pleased with the work I was doing. A few weeks after these visions, he started appearing to me as one of my longtime guides.)

Ceci told me about a shorter version of my healings with people in the markets. All I had to do was look into their eyes to know what energy to send them. Everyone on these outings had to be especially discreet. Sometimes the reaction from a villager was incredible, and they often found it difficult to remain poised until I passed by. Ceci explained that I seemed to float as I passed each vendor's stall. Even my guards could tell something was happening; they developed a strong reverence for me and my path through the market. Those walks ended when a new guard was assigned. He was hard and had a reputation for his cruelty. He scrutinized every move I made. I learned later that he was a spy for one of my teachers. The teacher had become very jealous; he had known of my secret work for a long time, unsuccessfully trying to copy my techniques. Even after I showed him how to do them, he failed because he was not pure in thought.

Ceci paused before telling me that it was time to begin that work again. People would come to my house for healing work, and others would be healed through daily contact in public places. Some would be healed by a simple look that sent them one of my healing stars. The colors were important; I used white with bits of color on the edges and in the center. Only some people could see these stars. All I had to do was give a conscious command to allow healer friends see these stars. They were my protectors, my team.

Ceci knew I was curious about the paintings, but she showed me more of my old living space. The large wooden table that I had used to create my paintings had lots of colors dabbed around it. Logs for the large fireplace lay to one side. She told me that she had assisted in keeping the space in order for me. I was not a neat person and would just let things stack up. I had no trouble with the disarray. I always found what I was looking for—as long as Ceci did not try to straighten things up after me. There were times when she could no longer resist the clutter, and her good deeds were always followed by some frustrated excitement while I searched for something that had been moved.

The large space was divided between sleeping and working. It was kept simple with very little furnishings even though I could have had much more. Most nights I did not sleep much. Ceci would come in some mornings to find me secretly working on a painting or writing in one of my journals. Most of the paintings were of small stars in different colors. During the daytime, and sometimes after being up all night working on my personal projects, my younger brother would send for me to work on a painting. There were many paintings of him. He liked my energy and wanted to be near me. He felt better when he spent time around me. He did not try to understand it or why it happened with everyone who spent time around me. All he knew was that he did not want to share me with others. That was why he kept such a tight hold on my activities. The effect of the energy on him was like a drug or alcohol addiction. The only legitimate way he could feel close was when he sat for a painting.

Ceci described a particular visit to the village for a day of healing. Henry had screened the villagers very carefully to keep out anyone who might report back to the king. There were five people coming that day. The tailor had some new fabric for the fitting of a new dress. While there, the following people had healings:

- *An elderly woman who had difficulty straightening her back. She was bent over in a great deal of pain. You sat in a chair while she stood in front of you. You closed your eyes, asked for the one above to guide you, and your hands went to the body—the left hand on her lower back, the other hand about three inches in front of her belly. I saw energy pulsing from about a foot above your head, through your body, down your arms, strongest on the left. The right hand balanced and caught the energy being pulsed in the left. You instructed the woman to breathe as if she was breathing the same energy in through the top of her head, pulling it down into her belly, and then to breathing it all out from her bellybutton. Another ball of energy appeared above the woman's head, light pulsing into her body, down her back into your hands. The two pulsing beams of energy met, and all the energy expanded to encompass the both of you. She gradually stood straight and was pain free for the rest of her life.*

- *The next person was a young boy. He had broken his leg and it was healing badly. He knew you from the market and was very happy to see you. You placed your hands around the injured part of his leg, energy channeled through the both of you, and with a little pop, the leg straightened and healed completely within two days.*

- *A man was brought to you with sickness and dizziness. He had not been able to eat for some time. You worked on his head (tumor) and then work on his upper left chest (lung tumor). He was well for a time, but he became ill again and died. This was an example of faith. He was always discounting your work to himself and his family.*

- *The last two for that day were babies. The twin sisters were not gaining weight. The mother's milk had not been enough, and they were being given goat's milk. They still did not gain weight with the extra milk. You knew they had been born too early; they barely had the strength to breathe. You looked at them with a very deep sense of love and put a hand on each one's belly. They immediately became calm, and they rested well for several hours. After that, they ate hungrily; within a few days, they began to gain weight.*

Ceci began to tell me a story about my brother, the prince. After returning to my rooms following a full day of healings, my brother arrived to make arrangements for a new painting. He wanted the entire house in the background of this one, and he wanted me to get started right away. It was the time of year when there were not many sunny days; more often, there were lots of clouds with rain showers.

The conversation went along with his plan to get me alone in his coach. He was determined to have me as his own property in one way or another. He was never married. Women thought he was too pretty, or he thought the women were not pretty enough to be a compliment for him. He had been tall and very good looking, but he eventually became overweight, sloppy, and unpleasant to be around. He became angry when I avoided his advances. He knew he was wrong, always attempting an apology, but still making it clear he was jealous of my time in the village.

He grew obsessed with the idea that I might have a lover. This helped him decide to change the guards that took me into the village. I also discovered that he was quietly being manipulated by one of my teachers who had recognized my brother's passion for me and had coached him into instructing the new guards to watch every move I made, noting everyone I met.

During my next visit to the tailor, the guards insisted on staying in the room for the fitting and would not let me out of their sight. Three people were scheduled to see me that day; instead, I sent loving energy to each of them, knowing what needed healing. They were all well within a few days. Thus began my work with distant healings, and Henry continued compiling the list of people who asked for healing energy.

On the morning that I died in that lifetime, Ceci had come running into my room with the distressing news. I already knew the men were coming to kill me, but I was calm. She was in tears and did not understand why my teacher would have made these arrangements. She was afraid for me, but I told her to go home, reassuring her that all would be as it was meant to be. I already knew that the man who had ordered my death was one of my teachers. He had discovered my notebooks that described the healing sessions with the villagers. I had described abilities that he had not taught me. And he was unable to do any of that kind of work. He kept trying and failing. Each time he failed, he became more angry and frustrated with me.

His jealousy set into motion the decision to use his mystical influences on the guards, ordering them to kill me as a last effort to obtain my secrets. The anger tripped him because he had chosen my original guards to do his killing, thinking they would be punished for their deed. When they awoke from their trance, they realized what they had done and how it had been orchestrated. When he was exposed, he attempted to make me the scapegoat, but no one listened. My brother ordered him killed for his treason.

Ceci's final message from this other lifetime: "The important things now are your writings and your paintings. Write our conversations and use healing intentions in your paintings. Not all of them will be stars; faces will begin to appear, then sceneries, lots of color will be used, there will be lots of fun. Use colors and your rainbow rain meditation. The breath work through the crown will help your work with clients, especially the ones in a great deal of pain. Breathe out through your bellybutton instead of your feet, bring in colors with that breathing, and let it flow to your clients. And most important—*Paint to Remember.*"

The Present

Toward the end of 2011, I began attending a weekly painting class. The classes were small, and after a stressful start, my hands began to paint as if I were still in that other lifetime. All I had to do was take in a deep breath and exhale my intentions for that day's work. Something inside me knew that I was creating the opportunity to continue my soul's work that had been started so long ago. I seemed to go off into another world when I wrote, and I began having the same experience with painting. My time spent writing and painting felt like being home, and I have welcomed every minute of being able to do what I love.

Cabin in the Woods

The Present

A girlfriend and I liked to keep track of the holistic fair schedule, especially searching out the fairs with vendors who offered natural gemstones. I found a listing for an expo that was new to us. They had a more diverse variety of vendors with offerings that included different kinds of healers, music, artwork, and handmade jewelry.

My friend was not able to go with me that weekend, but I had a compelling urge to attend and made the two-hour drive myself. I had just started my walk through the vendor aisles when I stopped at the opening to one of the lecture rooms. A big man with a long, gray beard was telling the intriguing story of his near death experience and his survival on a stretcher outside the morgue. He had been run over by a truck at a rainy intersection in Houston and had been pronounced dead on his way to the hospital.

I followed him to his booth where he had a display of handmade quartz pendants, wands, and music CDs created from his memories of the other side. I watched him as he gently picked out quartz wands or pendants for his customers. I was fascinated with the ease and warmth of his connection with other people.

As I turned to continue my tour of the expo, he took hold of my arm, silently asking me not to move. I felt rooted to the spot. I watched him reach over, pick out one of his pendants, and hand it to me. He told me that one day I would be playing music on a keyboard similar to the music on his CDs. The most unforgettable moment was when he hugged me as we parted. He gently wrapped his arms around me as if we were very old and very dear friends, holding his light grip for more than a few seconds. The warmth of his touch was something I had never experienced.

He made such an impression with me that I continued to follow this expo's website, watching for the next time he was scheduled as a vendor. For his next lecture, he told us about being an illustrator for Disney and his desire to have his life story made into a movie. He also talked about the new children that were arriving. He looked at me and described the special books they would need. We seemed to connect; both of us knew exactly what he meant. I felt a little overwhelmed, but part of me knew what he was talking about—it just wasn't quite clear in my head yet. (About a year later, I did write some chakra energy exercises for children. I also had a story published in a community magazine describing how I taught my four-year-old granddaughter to ask her angels for help.)

The last time I saw this big bear of a man, my friend was finally able to come with me. We listened to him tell his near-death story, and then he described a movie he had recently seen. The movie was about some unknown force that was testing the connections between a parent and their child.

While looking directly at me, he said, "And we both wished we had not gone to that movie." He did not explain to the audience what he meant, but I immediately answered yes. I knew instantly what he was talking about. The movie had an accident scene in it that filled the entire movie screen with shattering glass. My friend had sat next to me during that movie and was very concerned when I nearly jumped out of the theater seat. That scene took me back to my own near death-experience following an auto accident.

The warmth of his presence was still with me. His words gave me an opportunity to more deeply recognize my own spiritual connections with the world around me. The lingering sensations of that hug were like a deepening in the oneness that continues to gain strength in my own spiritual journey.

Journal Notes of a Relevant Other Lifetime

Timothy's parents had repeatedly told him that they were on the greatest adventure of their lives. They were part of a wagon train with several other families to find new homes in the West. He grew tired of the adventure and pouted when he heard those words repeated. Sometimes the trip was not very much fun. His mother was always fretting about where he was, making sure she could see him at all times.

They had been traveling with a group of wagons for more than a month; for a five-year-old, it felt like a very, very long time. He did find some fun getting dirty, knowing he would not have to bathe right away. His mother sometimes followed him with a wet towel, but that was okay compared to the full scrubbing he would get in a bath. Water was precious, and it did not take him long to figure out he would not have to have scrubbings like the ones he received when they had lived in the city. His mother tried to keep him from getting too dirty by making him stay in the wagon most of the time.

Everyone had been up before dawn, and his mother had been busy with the family that lived in the wagon ahead of them. Timothy had been put down for a morning nap, and his mother thought he was asleep. He had been peeking out under the wagon cover, watching for the right time to quietly climb out the back. He slept a little, but soon he was up and out of his covers, scrambling over the back of the wagon while the adults were busy. The look on his face made it clear that he was looking for some kind of new adventure. There were rocks to check out, strange insects to watch, and the occasional lizard to chase.

When he found a creek, he looked over his shoulder to see if his mother was coming. Playing in the water was something he knew his mother would not like. The water was very cold, but he had fun playing at the bank, turning rocks over to see what kind of creatures skipped away. He wandered into the brush and began putting brightly colored rocks in his pockets. When he heard the noise of horses and wagons, he began running. His heart was pounding as he thought about his mother's anger. He ran and did not stop—even when his special rocks and sticks fell out of his pockets. There was so much dust that he began to choke. Their wagon was gone, and he can barely make out the shadow of the last one that was now moving too fast for him to catch. No one heard his cries through the noise. The dust settles and the air becomes very quiet. He was frightened and stands there with a mixture of dirt and tears caked on his face.

After several hours, Timothy heard the sound of a horse moving through the brush. He thought of the big horse that his father rode while his mother handled the wagon. He was shocked a second time when he did not see his father. Instead, in front of him was a huge man on top of an equally sized horse. He had what looked like lots of dead animals tied around his neck. They stared at each other for a few moments. The man had no idea where this child might have come from, and it took him a few minutes to figure out what he had to do next.

The man finally reached for the boy's hand, pulling him up to sit in front of him on a cushion of animal skins. Timothy thought that the man looked like a bear, and he made a face at the awful smell. Over time, Timothy became used to the strong odor of the animal skins tied around the man's neck. They were on the horse for two full days, stopping only once to build a fire and eat, before arriving at the man's home. The large one-room cabin had a big fireplace and stove with a large pot for brewing coffee. Against the wall next to the fireplace was a bed covered with a large piece of fur.

The man sorted through some smaller furs and placed one on the floor. He signaled Timothy that this would be his space in the room. Later on, he was given a small trunk to save trinkets that he had found. The old man rarely spoke, talking to the boy only when giving the occasional orders that taught him how to help around the cabin.

Timothy soon became familiar with his surroundings and the trails that the old man traveled throughout the year. Their routine involved setting traps, cleaning the animals that were caught, eating and drying the different meats, and then curing the skins that would one day be taken into town for sale. Sometimes it was very strenuous work. In the spring, there was a trip to the city to sell the skins, get a hot bath, and shave. Sometimes they purchased new clothing or blankets; one time there was a special purchase of a few books so Timothy could learn how to read and write.

Blond with blue-green eyes, Timothy grew up with very little verbalizing and even less touching from this wilderness man (known only as Joe by those who knew him). Timothy grew to be a lanky young man with a soft, gentle temperament. As he grew older, Timothy began making plans to leave. He felt ready to be on his own and had become curious about the world outside of the mountains. He did not have any formal schooling, but he knew that to be successful in handling his finances, he must learn to read and write a little better.

About the time Timothy began thinking about the future, Joe went into town for a few supplies. A friend of his kept a collection of old newspapers to give him; in one of the more recent copies, there was a story of a couple who had settled in a nearby city. The man was now running for mayor, and the paper had written about the couple's travels from the East Coast and about their loss of a son on that journey. The old man seemed to know instantly that his young companion might be their son.

The boy was nearly a man. How could he be sure this was the same boy? How could he not investigate? His heart ached for what he must do, but he decided to say nothing until he figured out how to handle this news. Joe returned to the cabin and took some time to get used to the information. Joe began going out by himself to reset the traps. This gave him time to adjust to the idea that his young companion would be leaving him soon. He tried to argue with himself. The boy was just some child he had found on the trail. He had not worked hard at creating any great friendship; he had just made sure that the young man was fed and clothed, kept busy during the day, and stayed warm at night. He realized that he had grown fond of Timothy; the thought of not having him around was beginning to hurt.

Timothy had been thinking about his own plans to leave. He was not sure if he would return after their next trip to town or just pack up and leave from the cabin. He had already collected all of his personal things in his small trunk. It included the clothing that he had been wearing when he was lost. That choice was taken from him when Joe announced they had some talking to do. He was going to make plans with an old friend in town about giving the boy a job and a place to stay until he could begin making his own financial decisions. He even gave Timothy a new leather pack for all of his things. The boy was totally surprised by this change of events, and his heart raced with thoughts of new things to learn—and maybe going to school. The days before that trip were even quieter than those before the announcement.

Then the bear attacked. Neither one of them made it to town that year. The old man had found Timothy when he returned from checking his traps. He buried him in a grove of trees near a stream that had always been Timothy's favorite spot. If the boy was missing, the old man always knew where to look—next to that stream with clear sight of the cabin above him and a view of a lake below with the mountains surrounding it all.

My Potential Future

The last few years had been very good to me, and it was time to begin working on that phrase in my head "my cabin in the woods." During the last few years at my corporate job, I often told my fellow workers that I was going to retire to my cabin in the woods. They never understood it because I could not tell them where it was—only that I knew it was out there waiting for me. I decided that it was the time to do something about it.

At first, the large number of listings presented to me was overwhelming. The Realtor had been highly recommended, but with my list of requirements, she had not been able to find anything that felt close to what I had been visualizing. We had reviewed a number of listings at her office and finally agreed to see a few. She must have thought I was nuts when I said no to each house as soon as we stopped in front of them. I had begun to wonder if she really understood what I wanted or if I was just not communicating the images in my head.

I was ready to change Realtors when I reluctantly agreed to see one more piece of property. She explained that the house had been empty for some time, and her client had recently reduced his price for a quick sale. She admitted some hesitation in showing me the place because she did not feel it would be a good fit for me. She described it as a large piece of property, set back into a wooded area with a simple one-room cabin. She also suggested that the price might be one of those "too good to be true" kind of things, adding that I would be the first of her clients to see the property.

She had no idea what kind of surprise was in store for us. We were on a gravel driveway that sloped upward, circling through heavy brush and pine trees. The house was not even in our view when I felt a tingling sense of anticipation. The road turned again and, through the trees, my first view of the cabin was incredible. It was exactly as I had envisioned many years earlier while working my corporate job. I was silent as she showed me through the cabin, letting her talk about it and listening to her hesitations about how I might be able to fix this and change that. To me, nothing appeared to need fixing. I didn't want to change a thing. Everything in the cabin appeared to be recently updated and was in very good condition. I was on the verge of saying yes when we walked out the back door. Stretched out before us was a beautiful ridge of mountains; below the trail, a lake shimmered in the evening sun. It was a breathtaking find, and we signed papers the same day.

The cabin in the woods became my home away from home. Each morning, I slipped into a comfortable cotton dress and sat down at my desk filled with tablets, pens, pencils, and a laptop computer. Some time was spent journaling before working with the computer. My project on that trip was to get more organized with the notes about my current manuscript. I had a lot of work to do before the weather got colder and the snow started falling. When I was there, I was able to seclude myself away from the activities of my retreat center where I lived and worked with other healing practitioners who resist the "retirement" label.

My little dog whined to remind me that it was time for breakfast. She knew I was working, but I had spoiled her with a hot meal each morning and it was past our usual breakfast break. A few hours later, she reminded me when it was time to take another break. I pulled on my jacket and slipped a sweater over her shorthaired body for a walk in the woods.

Sometimes we take the path to the lake, and other times we take the path into town. I noticed all the changes that had occurred since my spring visit and sighed after taking in a deep breath of late October. I loved the smell of the fallen leaves that filled the woods. The noises were different and quieter because many of the birds had gone to warmer climates. Now I listened to a different layer of forest noise. An hour later, we returned to the cabin. My thoughts were refreshed, and I was ready for the next few hours of writing. My little dog curled up at my feet for her first nap of the day; she would not move again until she sensed some creature invading her outdoor space.

The Present

One of the few items that I had from my high school days was a clay figure of a woman in a long dress that I created during art class in my senior year. From day one of getting that assignment, I could see her standing at the top of a grassy rise with the wind behind her blowing her scarf and causing her skirt to billow out around her. I also had the impression that she was looking back in the direction of where she had been.

Over the years, her head had broken off, and I had done a really poor job of gluing it back together. I looked at it and wondered what had I been thinking by being so sloppy with the glue. A few years ago, I found a soft piece of maroon ribbon to tie around her neck to hide the break. She had a special place on my desk; when I looked at her, I was reminded of that image on the hillside. While receiving information for this chapter, I recognized that my little clay statue was a representation of Ceci. In this chapter, she was Timothy's mother, and she was with me as a guide in this lifetime to help me remember.

Cliff Jumper

The Present

The first time I put the ending to this story on paper, I had been in bed for only few minutes and could not stop tossing and turning. Words and pictures were flashing around in my head like clips from a movie, and there was no going back to sleep. As I wondered where it was coming from, I felt a strong urge to get out of bed. All I could hear were the words for an introduction and an ending related to my journal notes about another lifetime. It was so clear in my head that I wrote until it was out of me. I put the notes away to let them settle a bit and was finally able to sleep.

Two days later, I woke up late and did not understand why I was so tired. I had slept a solid seven hours, which was kind of unusual. I rarely slept straight through any night. I was suddenly curious about an old friend's wedding date. After doing some research, I was not surprised to find a wedding announcement showing that the event had occurred the previous evening. I took a deep breath and closed my eyes to see one of my guides dancing and laughing at me. She told me that the two of us had been out all night to celebrate closure for this learning experience.

My Potential Future

I was celebrating my sixty-fifth birthday by taking myself and a friend to the gulf beaches of Mexico. I had taken a leisurely walk through the shops and stopped at an outdoor café to rest my feet and read a chapter of one of my favorite novels.

When I heard a surprised voice say hello, I looked up to see an old friend and former healthcare provider. He nodded curiously toward the book. I smiled, remembering the many conversations about other books we had had together while I was in his care. It had been almost six years. I noticed that he still walked with a slight limp, but the old shoulder trauma didn't seem to be giving him any trouble. He introduced his wife and a young lady who was about three years old. The last time I had been in his office, he had told me about his wedding plans and honeymoon. I also remembered when he had first met his wife, and I was reminded why my visits to him gradually stopped.

I invited them to sit with me for lunch. The mother and the young lady looked tired, and they were more than ready to stop for a rest. Edward sat directly across from me, and Francine sat across to my right; Emily sat in a chair between them. We ordered lunch and began giving each other updates. I told them that I was only semi-retired, and this trip was about relaxing after having written a few books. The books had done very well, and I was taking a long-awaited break from writing, publishing and promoting. For the past five years, there had barely been time to fit in a few clients, a few lectures, and a few teaching engagements. This vacation was to help my energies regroup before heading to my cabin in the woods for some serious work on my next book.

Edward's business was doing very well. About four years earlier, he had moved into a new two-story building with a couple of other practitioners; their offices were full of clients every day. Francine only worked part-time so their daughter would not spend too much time with a sitter.

Emily fell asleep in her chair. Her face was a little flushed, and I was thinking that she might be overheated when her mom picked her up and moved her to her lap. Edward was telling me that they were on vacation—the first since their honeymoon six years earlier. They talked about that trip for a few moments and then let me know that this vacation was meant for relaxing, walking along the beaches, and eating whenever and whatever they felt like eating. They were fit and trim, indicating he still went to the gym five or six times a week. As we begin eating our lunch, they made it clear that their vacation plans included leaving their diets behind as soon as they stepped onto the plane.

We ordered some coffee, and Francine asked me about how I knew Edward. I explained that I had been one of his patients following an auto accident. I told her that our work together had kept me from having any surgery, and I was forever grateful. He and I smiled at each other, and I think it triggered something in Francine because—in a curious fashion—she asked if I had been one of the many female clients that had developed a crush on her husband. She said that this dilemma had plagued him for a long time. I was not sure what might be going on with her question, but it was fun to watch his face redden. I smiled as I told her my story.

Yes, I had had the most glorious crush on this young man. And I say "young man" because he was several years younger than me and exactly one year older that my youngest brother (thoughts of which had not helped to discourage my feelings). It was the kind of crush that teenagers have in high school. And it was a wonderful experience with absolutely no regrets. We had the best conversations about current healing and spiritual books. I often thought that we had our own personal book club meeting each time I visited his office.

At the time, I am sure he knew how I felt because he eventually told me that many of his female clients developed a crush, adding that the cause for these situations was his good looks (imagine a young Robert Redford/Paul Newman type). I am sure that those goods looks had encouraged the long lines of young ladies waiting to meet him at the community holistic fairs each month. I hadn't stood in line, but I did grab a business card to make an appointment with him.

Several months later, during one of our appointments, he mentioned that he had already had a relationship with an older woman—and he had no plans of going there again. I felt humiliated and wished I was someplace else. My feelings must have been extremely obvious, and it was clear that he was tired of it. I realized that I needed to do some fast thinking. As soon as he was finished talking, I told him about a new singles group I had found—and my hopes of meeting someone. That day was a tough one, and it had been especially difficult to maintain my balance. I told Francine about the many times he had answered the phone when she called—and how excited he always was to speak with her.

Francine began laughing at us both. It was clear that she had found an opportunity to give her husband's ego a hard time, and she was enjoying every minute of it. For her to bring it up so easily indicated that Edward must still have clients falling madly in love with him. While I was telling my story, he had been turning all shades of red. I decided to give him a break and changed the subject.

I asked him if he still liked the thought of hooking his toes over the edge of cliffs. His eyes brightened, and we talked about the extreme vacations he had attended—and recommended to me. We both laughed about hooking our toes on the edge of a cliff and leaning out as far as the cables would allow. It was perhaps the most exhilarating experience of my life, and I had always appreciated his recommendation.

Then I changed the subject again by asking him a "what if" question. What if he lived on a piece of property that overlooked a cliff; and, what if there was a big tree standing near the edge with a long rope hanging from one of the strongest branches. Would he grab the rope and swing out over the edge of the cliff as far as the rope would swing?

He did not think twice; he said, "Yes, in a heartbeat."

His energy expanded as he imagined himself jumping onto that swing. I remembered our first meeting when I had seen the old injury in his left hip. My professional work involved intuitively recognizing these kinds of injuries, but I did not offer any kind of information when I first met people. I waited for an opening that invited me to tell people what I had seen.

In his case, it took six weeks for him to describe falling from a swing when he was three years old. I did not tell him anything; I had already seen how he had injured his hip in a very different fall.

Journal Notes of a Relevant Other Lifetime

Two young people, each born into wealthy landowner families, had been betrothed since early childhood. Their parents saw their union as fortifying the riches of both families for future generations. The properties were located near Greece, overlooking the banks of the Mediterranean. The very proper young lady was very much in love with the young man, but he acted like an unruly child. He was careless with his time and everything he touched. On the day before their wedding, she was attempting to create an atmosphere of dignity in the hours leading up to the ceremony. He had been out all week wildly riding his horse and celebrating with his friends.

She walked down a path to the fields that overlooked the water. At the end of the field was a large tree that looked as if it had been there for centuries. Severe storms had taken many of its branches. From one strong limb, a single rope hung with a board tied at its end. When someone pushed hard enough, they could swing out over the edge of the cliff. If they were brave enough, they could look down at the rocks below. She had never done it, and her heart nearly stopped every time she saw her betrothed get on the swing. He always cheered when he swung out over the edge.

When she saw him heading toward it, she called out to him, begging him to stop. He paid her no attention. He started pulling and pushing the rope harder and harder as he moved back and forth. He was standing in the seat and holding onto the rope with just one arm. It was frightening for her to watch. Stillness came over them both when they heard the branch of the tree begin to crack. Before the rope could swing him back over land, the branch broke, and the young man flew out and away from the cliff to his death. The young lady stood in shock, and tears began to fall. Her grief turned to anger over the way he had left her. She had been so in love with him. How could he have been so careless?

It was years before she was married. After turning several potential suitors away, her parents were insistent. They were getting older and demanded that she marry someone who would care for her when they were gone. Within a few months, she married a gentle, caring man from Greece. He grew to love her dearly, helping her to eventually open up and return his love.

Back to My Potential Future

As I came out of my daydream, Edward and Francine were standing up to leave. Emily had awakened, and she was keeping them very busy. They mentioned reservations for an event on the other side of town, and they had little time to get back to the hotel to get ready. It was nice to see Edward again and to see him so happy.

I did not voice my thoughts and never told Edward about the past life memory of this young couple. Early in our working relationship, it seemed as if he had believed in multiple lifetimes, but later, he didn't. I did not tell him any of my stories or about the injuries from other lifetimes that I often saw in him. There seemed to be a few synchronicities in our lifetimes together. The most important was to understand why I had that crush on Edward. As I resolved my feelings, I recognized it as closure for the unrequited love in the loss of my future husband from that Greek lifetime. I also understood that I was not destined to be with him—not then and not this time either. As soon as I figured this out, a huge emotional piece of that crush was gone.

I checked the clock in the café and realized it was time to return to my hotel room. I was going to dinner with someone that I did not remember ever having had a past life experience. He was such a sweetheart.

The Present

One of the benefits of being a member of a healing group was working with a teacher from Europe. Ronnie was an in-law of one of our team members who had a diverse healing practice that included releasing emotional blocks from the spine, meridians, and internal organs. Our group always looked forward to his visits because we had a firsthand opportunity to learn Ronnie's techniques, and he often had something new to show us.

During one visit, I sponsored one of his workshops at my house. That night, we had a nice sized group crowded into the den, and the members of our group stood in the doorways. The first exercise was for releasing the emotions related to one or two vertebra of the spine. When it was my turn, Ronnie stopped at T4, telling me that there was some old bitterness in my heart. He seemed surprised because, in all our previous work together, he had not seen the issue. When the release work was complete, I felt something lift from my heart area.

During a break in the exercises, we had a discussion on reincarnation and past lives. I found it curious that comments revolved around people who did not believe in other lifetimes. Ronnie stated that these people were full of fear, and they were simply blocking the learning experience that could be achieved in each lifetime. I thought of how Edward had fit that description.

Early in our professional relationship, he had described some of his personal spiritual events and about being told by a visiting shaman that he had a hugely important life purpose that had not been fulfilled in a past lifetime due to fear. During one of our last meetings, he made it clear that he no longer believed in other lifetimes.

As for the classes with Ronnie, I had moved a couple of times and no longer had a connection with that healing group. Several months later, I learned that he had moved to an island in the Mediterranean.

Reconnecting with My Healing Tools

The Present

I stopped at one of my favorite metaphysical gift stores for a fresh supply of incense and a bundle of white sage. Before heading to the checkout counter, I turned toward the bookshelves. *Should I take a look today?* Many of the books that I had already collected had not been read and I hesitated before making any new purchases. To help in this task, I began keeping a "want" list with the idea that I would purchase only from that list or not at all. Book lovers might know that this plan sometimes works and sometimes does not. That afternoon, I recognized the author's name on a new display in the back of the store. The book included some of his channeling sessions with an archangel plus a description of the energies at sacred sites he had visited.

The next day was Sunday, and during that quiet afternoon, I took the time to get comfortable with this off-the-list purchase. After reading through several chapters, I became very relaxed and felt myself drift into a meditative state. The entertainment center and television across the room faded, and a window opened to show me another room that was definitely some place very distant. The dark space and its gray stone walls reminded me of a cave or cellar. To the right of a dark doorway or hall, a large, roughly finished wood table was positioned in the center of the room.

Suddenly, a great sadness descended on me, and tears filled my eyes. I had an overwhelming sensation of being reunited with long lost friends. I felt as if I was in the room, walking around the table with my hands lightly touching—almost caressing—the items on the table. To the left were stacks of leather-bound journals filled with layers of handwritten papers. To the right was a neatly folded piece of dark fabric. In the center were several items that I couldn't quite see or feel. I remembered what the room meant, and why these things were on the table. There was no indication of the time or place as the memories of that lifetime flooded back.

I was being shown some tools that I had hidden. In that lifetime, I had given up a part of myself. Most importantly, I had given up the ability to help others heal. I felt immense sorrow and guilt in this action. I began to recognize that, in my current lifetime, I was free to access this information—and I could begin using these tools again without any fear. I finished the meditation wiping the tears from my face.

Journal Notes of a Relevant Other Lifetime

During a writing meditation about that lifetime of hiding my healing tools, I wrote that I was about four years old when I began remembering the symbols. I was almost eleven when I began to fully understand how to use them. By the time I was twelve, I had begun remembering the many other lifetimes of using the same symbols—and how I had suffered for doing the work of a healer.

I am that twelve-year-old who was overwhelmed by the memories of repeated torture and death for doing the healing work. In that lifetime, I wanted something different. I wanted a long life. I wanted a partner, and I especially wanted to have children. With a great sense of sorrow and guilt, I decided to hide these tools, to not practice my gifts, and to not be known as a healer.

Shortly after my twelfth birthday, I began looking for a place to hide those tools safely with the hope of being able to use them again in some other lifetime. In the hundred-year-old estate where my father worked, there were many unused rooms. There was also a section that had never been used during the many years my family worked for the family. My father had always been cautioned to stay away from that part of the estate, and he had given me the same instructions. On several occasions, my curiosity prevailed, and I had gone exploring. This time, I knew exactly which room to use.

During the next meditation, there was more information about the items on the table. I was walking around the table in the room. I felt a deep knowing that I could begin using these tools again without any fear. For a few minutes, I looked through the journals, and then I reached for the folds of dark fabric on the other side of the table. It was a cloak that had been used to protect me and make me invisible. Its hood draped around my neck and easily covered my entire body. There was comfort in remembering that it was a cloak of protection. No one could see me or tap into my strength when I wore it. A voice told me to use the cloak thoughtfully, carefully.

"When you feel your energies being threatened, imagine the cloak covering you from head to toe with your face in its shadow. More meditation is required for the books and a new tablet for notes as you read from them. About the other items on the table—mostly jewelry and crystals, some of which you have already retrieved in this lifetime—the brown calcite, the two crystals, the twins."

After that meditation, I decided to review one of my old journals. I found notes about a person I had worked with that was always attempting to tap into my space. When I felt him in that moment, I knew that he was trying to tap into my space again. He was relentless, but a voice told me to put on my cloak. I spread the cloak around the room while I worked. The top of my head tingled, but—after a few prayers—I was back on track with the writing. There was heaviness in my arms. I had learned that this heaviness was an indication of others who want to communicate through me. There seemed to be much that needed to be relayed to others. I received confirmation from a tingle on the back of my head.

The voice said, "Yes, you were really here with us. We have waited a long time—just the right time—and now the work begins. Set your standards for training others. Yes, he keeps trying and can't get through. He realizes his days were numbered. We laugh in this.

"About the cloak, you were given this by God's angels when it became apparent that you must hide yourself and your work. This began many lifetimes ago—not in the first one, but in our realization that you could not survive for long in *any* lifetime. Your work was—and is—very important. The cloak was made of silk and linen; its colors were dark red and brown. It covered you well; it also hid the light and brightly colored clothing that you often wore. The fabric was dense and heavy to the touch—but it was light when you placed it over your shoulders. The draping hood held your long hair back and swung around your body about three inches below your feet. It usually fell flat on the ground, but sometimes it seemed to melt into the surface where you stood. Those times you were truly invisible. People could walk right by you and not see you. The only problem was that if someone accidently touched you, you were automatically discovered. This often had dire results.

"About the books—they were journals of your healing techniques. There were not that many, one book for each technique. They were not complicated. Most of each journal was about how you used them with individuals and the results. You will do the same here. Keep records on each individual, get testimonials.

"You danced for the fun of it, mostly rhythmical steps to no one's style, only your direction. As you danced, your light shined rays of color that only a few could see. People were mesmerized, and you were often gone from your stage before their wits returned. This was similar to what happens when you do Tai Chi."

The Present

For each of the old journals, I created a new journal with a drawing of the symbol and a description of how each one was used. When I finished writing about all nine symbols, I placed them on a large poster. The last symbol was like the spokes of a wheel with a space for all the other symbols at the ends of the spokes. Soon after I finished that poster, I was guided to put the new journals and the poster away. I was not to use them.

Over the next few months, new symbols began floating in front of me. Five new symbols appeared, and I was directed by my angels to freely share them with others and give them away as bookmarks. Individually, each symbol represented a contributing aspect of unconditional love; each was to be defined by the owner's perception of unconditional love. The cards also serve as reminders that we were all very important in this universe. (These symbols are used on the cover.)

Several months later, still feeling a faint sense of guilt and sorrow associated with hiding the original symbols, I asked for a healing session with two friends. They helped me travel back to that room, to that part of me that hid the tools. The young lady in her working clothes looked at me as if she had been waiting for me. She came around the table to greet me; before we touched, she was sobbing so hard that I began crying with her. She realized that my arms were wrapped around her. I was consoling her, letting her know that I had found her tools—*our* tools. She dried her tears and began dancing and twirling around the room. The cape around her shoulders flew in the air over the table. She was so light on her feet, so happy, and joy filled us both.

When I thought the session was ending, two more scenes appeared. First, there was another image of myself running, being chased. I was slender and wore tight black leather breeches, a shirt and vest, gloves, boots, and a short cape. I wore a hat, and a black scarf was tightly wrapped my long blonde hair. I kept running and looking back, terrified, somehow knowing that I would not get away this time. Then I saw myself crumpled on my back with my legs twisted under me.

The second scene was of a small child drawing the symbols in the air, playing with them as if they were toys. The next impression was that the child had been killed for trying to tell someone about them. When I awoke, I had the distinct feeling that the persecution for being a healer was over.

Missing the Boat

The Present

About once a year, one of my younger sisters likes to pester me about going on a cruise with her. This time, the highlight of her pleading was a cruise departing in six weeks from Galveston, Texas, not far from where I lived. She described several details in the hopes that I might change my mind. I made it clear that I had no interest in getting on a boat and going out to sea. Our conversation coincided with plans for my own important event. The cruise left on the same day I was scheduled to participate as a vendor in a wellness fair that I was determined to attend.

Six weeks later, I arrived early to set up my space at the fair. A wide variety of vendors were scheduled to be there, and I was looking forward to meeting all of them. I was especially interested in talking with two people I had not met before. It would be the first time to have my palms read, and this person had been doing this kind of work for several years. I was amazed by how much she was able to tell me about my life. She told me that it was time for me to move from my apartment and that I should move someplace where I could see the stars.

The second vendor was an intuitive who offered past life regression. My spiritual healing journey had not included any past life work. In fact, I had always avoided doing this kind of personal work. However, when the practitioner offered a session, I found myself immediately agreeable to his invitation. I felt a warm feeling that I could trust him, and we walked into another room away from the noise of the fair. This first session began a three-year journey of looking for other lifetimes.

Journal Notes of a Relevant Other Lifetime

I saw myself in an early English era where I was a servant in a large expensive home. They were very strict with me, making sure of where I was at all times. I was dressed well—even though I was not a member of the family. My parents had worked for this family for many years before they had been killed in an accident the prior year. The owner of the house had taken me in out of respect for the work they had done for him, but he made it clear that I was still an orphan boy who had been taken in by the richest family in town. The family owned the area's largest shipbuilding port. His only son was in charge of all the vessels and managed the shipments of goods that were traded between several countries. I was very curious about the ships and their distant ports.

I was especially anxious because I had a secret appointment to meet someone. I double-checked my appearance in a large, ornate mirror near the main entrance of the house. I was a young man about eleven years old. My clothing was tailored in shades of gold and brown. I was preparing to meet someone with the intention of leaving this family behind. I had made sure that all of my chores were completed, and I was only waiting for my master to become distracted enough by his guests that I could leave without being noticed. They were taking a long time to start their meeting, and I was afraid that I would be late for my own meeting.

I met a ship's captain after one of his meetings with my master. There had been issues with scheduling a future cargo. My master and the owner of the cargo were very concerned. The captain—who was in charge of a fleet of ships—had a reputation for being more than a little reckless, and this cargo was of great value.

Every once in a while I would be in town on an errand. I would watch the loading and unloading of the ship; and, for a chance to talk with its captain. He had noticed my interest in his ships. He was an imposing figure, tall with long dark hair that he pulled back into a ponytail. He wore a long red coat with gold buttons, gray trousers, and a shiny pair of high-topped black boots. He also had a plumed black hat.

When I finally gathered the courage to ask if I could come with him on one of his journeys, he told me that he would be leaving the next day. If I really wanted to go with him, I had to be there on time because he would not be able to wait for me. My own timing was important because I knew that there was no going back when I left the house.

When my master appeared fully distracted, I ran all the way down the dirt road into town. My heart was beating as if it was ready to come out of my chest, and I could hardly breathe. I almost tripped over my feet when I saw that the ship was gone and was nowhere in sight. My next thought was that I would be in serious trouble with my master. By then, he would have discovered that I was missing, and thoughts of his warnings caused terror in me.

I was able to hide for a few days, knowing he had someone looking for me. I traded my clothing for something less conspicuous, but I was still discovered. When I was found, I was wearing black leather breeches, a shirt and vest, and a very old pair of high top black boots. My hat had fallen off while I was running, but a tightly tied black scarf had stayed around my hair. I kept running and looking back, terrified, somehow knowing that I could not get away. Then I fell, crumpling on my back with my legs twisted under me.

The Present

When I came out of the past life regression, I was asked to picture the person that the boy had missed at the dock. I was also asked to verify whether that person was represented in this lifetime. After saying yes, I was instructed to place a mask to represent the person's face from this lifetime over the other. They matched, indicating some unfinished business to be handled in this lifetime. I had already been feeling the potential for "missing the boat" with one of my current mentors.

Through personal healing work over the next several months, I discovered that I had been a servant in many lifetimes. In looking at a picture of one of my younger sisters I thought about how much she enjoys her cruise vacations. She had been that master and shipbuilder and had also been a father figure for me in other lifetimes. This helped explain the somewhat opposite dynamics of our relationship in this lifetime.

Victorian Pansies

The Present

For several weeks during the spring of 2010, I had asked—and sometimes pleaded—with the Universe to help me find and release whatever was keeping me from moving forward with my healing work. Part of my massage therapy work focused on helping clients release old trauma that had been stored in their bodies. Much of their trauma had been forgotten, but some of it was related to other lifetimes. The work was gentle and extremely beneficial for the willing client—and totally exhilarating for me. I considered myself a practitioner who could help others learn how to heal themselves, but I had begun to feel empty in my work. I recognized that it might be time for the healer to heal something within herself.

Knowing it was time for change, I decided to move. Before packing anything, I gave away half my library of books and several pieces of furniture. I moved to a state that required a massage therapy license to do any kind of healing touch which also meant going back to school. I completed the required additional hours for the new massage therapy license, but after several months, I was still not working. I became depressed about not doing the healing work and not being able to understand why this was happening.

I began asking the Universe to show me the issues of other lifetimes that were being played out in this lifetime—to show me what was directly related to my hesitation in moving forward. Before receiving that answer, I moved again to another state. In making that decision, I had pulled out a map and asked for insight to let my eyes stop in the area that would meet my highest good. My eyes quickly settled on the line between Arkansas and Missouri.

As my plans developed, I gradually focused on the southern part of Missouri, especially the Mark Twain National Forest. With the area picked out, I de-cluttered again, put household furnishings in storage, packed the car, and took a road trip. Three days later, I ended my trip in a small city that was reminiscent of the town where I had grown up.

After a few weeks, I settled into a new apartment and began looking for a job. I initially challenged myself by not making any attempts at transferring my massage therapy license and spent weeks looking for office work. When I started hearing a phrase that I had used while preparing to retire from the corporate world—"I deserve to do what I love to do, and I love doing what God intended me to do"—I submitted my paperwork to transfer my massage therapy license. I had the new license within a week. It felt so good to know that I could get back into that kind of work. A few weeks later, I was still not employed.

I stretched out in my bed for an afternoon nap. Instead of sleeping, I immediately felt the fabric of the dress worn by a woman from the Victorian era. The fabric felt precious to the young lady wearing it. I could see a small pattern of flowers on a violet background. The pattern in the fabric reminded me of the dark violet pansy stationery that I used to collect. There were soft white ruffles lining the inner layers of the sleeve at her wrists and on the collar. There was a hint of red in her light brown curly hair that had been pulled up tightly at the back of her head. I knew she was very wealthy, living alone on her family's estate. I felt her loneliness and her determination to survive on her own without anyone's help. Loneliness and having no one's help. Those last few words felt very familiar.

Journal Notes from a Relevant Other Lifetime

It was in the early 1720s; my name was Sarah. From a high-back upholstered chair, I looked out a large wall of windows over the properties that I had inherited from my father. My future husband had left me. I could still feel his anger as he denounced my intuitive skills as the work of the devil. I don't understand how we came together in the first place, and I am especially saddened that I could never convince him that the things I saw and heard were real. He was very influential in this town; he was an especially prominent figure with the political groups who had strong intentions of supporting his way through governmental positions.

Many knew him as someone who ensured that an individual's beliefs were beneficial for both him and the community. If your belief systems were not in line with his causes, your social life was very limited. With me, he was manipulative in a quiet, provocative way, making sure that I always spoke well of him. As for my beliefs, it took him a while, but when he fully understood the kind of conversations I had with my friends, he became afraid of what I might see in him. He was most afraid that I might tell others his secrets—even though I repeatedly tried to reassure him that was not how my insight worked. In his final tirade, he made it clear that he would suggest to others that I might tell all their secrets to the next person that came to see me. This effectively destroyed all the faith people had in me and my work. He had not gone so far as to call me a witch, but he definitely said something that made the townspeople avoid me.

I stayed home most days. I often looked out the windows, crying for the information I could not give to others, for the insightful confirmations I had given my friends, and for the fulfillment I received in knowing that I was of help to them. No one in my large circle of friends came to see me. For days at a time, I sat in the beautiful house surrounded by the gardens.

The only people around were those who maintained the house and property. Most of the workers and their families had been with my family for a long time. My parents had similar intuitive skills, and the families they employed had held a special reverence for those abilities. The workers were aware of what I could do and seemed to have not lost their faith in me, but they had become quiet when they were around me.

When I could bear the loneliness no longer, I packed a bag and traveled to another city to enjoy the crowds in a large hotel. The trips gave me a chance to be around people who did not know me. It also created an opportunity to connect with others like me. These people always seemed to find me; they always knew that I could see things in a similar fashion. Sometimes we had a few meetings to talk and support each other's work. When I had a clear picture of who they were and what they could see or hear, I seemed to unconsciously find some way to reject them. Sadly, this rejection sometimes occurred in an exceptionally unflattering way—many times in front of others in their community.

I felt out of control when this happened. I knew when my time was finished in a new place because I would have already packed my bag and would be ready to settle the hotel bill. I was punishing myself with what I did to others—as if I were passing on my pain. I quickly exited—as if I were running for my life.

As for the hotel, I had always paid cash up front and used a different name so that I could leave quickly and not be traced back to my hometown. When I returned home, it took several days to get over my distress about the way I had hurt new friends.

Katherine J. Keilman

The Present

I sighed deeply as I read those notes again. Her loneliness felt so familiar. I thought how a teacher or mentor could also be a parent, a mother/father figure, or some adult from your childhood. When I took a closer look, I saw that I had experienced a similar situation caused by someone who had a significant impact upon my life. They had been afraid of what I might say to others and I had been intimidated into silence. There was no one to turn to because everyone around me was afraid of the repercussions that they might have had to endure from that strong adult figure. My only relief was to move far away.

In this lifetime, I only remembered a few of my early childhood memories. Most of the good memories had been stifled by the traumatic ones and remained hidden until I was in my fifties. Through personal healing, I discovered that I was well aware of my psychic skills from a very early age. At four years old, I tried to tell an adult about the things I was seeing and hearing. The visions were scary, and I was frightened. When that adult realized what might happen if I were to talk to someone else, they became fearful and made it clear that I was dreaming things sent by the devil. I still see that person's face in front of me—and the fear in their voice. They reminded me on more than one occasion that I must not allow those kinds of thoughts to linger. I promised not to repeat what I saw or heard. Somewhere deep inside, even though I knew this was wrong, I still made the decision to not see the pictures or hear the words. I learned quickly to put them out of my head. It became easy to understand the importance of what I was told when there was also the memory of a painful grip on my shoulders as I was shaken into submission.

Throughout my childhood, I often felt separated. I always felt that I was being watched more closely than my siblings. To keep tabs on me, I was often given extra chores. This did not sit well with my siblings because extra chores meant extra allowance. The hardest part was trying to understand why close friendships between siblings did not exist. We were well into our thirties before any of us discovered the manipulations designed to prevent lifelong friendships, all aimed at keeping family secrets.

After almost eight years of rediscovery, I had remembered many of the fearful events between the ages of four through eleven. Learning the details of other lifetimes—sometimes including multiple lifetimes—helped me uncover unresolved issues that had followed me into this lifetime. Those memories have helped me understand why I chose to live away from family. I have forgiven key players involved in creating that childhood fear. I appreciate their company during my visits, and I have even had forgiving conversations with those who have already passed.

As for finding work, I remind myself to concentrate on doing what I love to do. Someone said, "When you do what you love, the money follows." For now, I enjoy a deep sense of freedom in being able to connect with those who would like my intuitive advice. While doing some hospice volunteering a couple of years ago, I discovered a different technique for giving readings. My hand sketches a colorful drawing for the client while we talk. This creates a little distraction for clients instead of using cards. We talk about what was going on in their life at the moment, and the drawing focuses on a current issue—usually something that has not yet come up in conversation. This creates something tangible that the client takes home with them.

The Wizard

About two years into my research on other lifetimes, I recognized a trend. The most significant male figures that have influenced me in this lifetime were in their forties. I began having flashes of one memory where all of us had been together in one very early lifetime.

When I sat for meditation to gain insight into these flashes, I immediately had a vision of standing in a wizard's cloak before a roomful of students. There was no sense of past or present. I stood at one end of the room with my hands gently feeling the folds of the thick fabric around me. I felt as if I had traveled into this body and was remembering the feeling of the cloak for the first time.

As I looked around, I felt the multiple lifetimes that all of us in the room had experienced together. It felt normal to have the sensation that the lifetimes were current and alive at the same time. I was looking at my students through the eyes of an elderly teacher, and I had the sense that I was still that teacher. I also knew that—for all of us—this was a vision of our first lifetime together.

Several weeks later, during a meeting with a group of intuitive friends, the talk turned to a mutual instructor. Not all of us felt the same about this guy, and I drifted to my memory of the wizard. I sighed in disappointment. The person we were talking about happened to be one of those students. He was tall and attractive with dark brown hair.

As my young apprentice, he had always tested me. I knew that he still had not learned his lessons. In this lifetime, I had been his student. When I became aware that he had manipulated me, I let it go on for way too long. I finally reached a point where I would not put up with it any longer. My friends did not understand why I was no longer loyal to him. The conversation continued, and I stayed quiet as others spoke up about the healing technique we had learned from him and how we were going to offer those sessions to clients.

In the past, I had been defensive about why I no longer wished to work with him, attempting to make the others in the group see my perspective. This night, I heard my voice complimenting his work. Something in me felt finished with him, and there was no more defending myself or my work—to him or to anyone else.

A few nights after the meeting, I opened my eyes in my darkened bedroom and saw some friendly figures perched on the blades of the ceiling fan. Their appearance was so vivid and real. I acknowledged their presence without giving them any further attention, but my sleep was not restful for the next two nights. I soon recognized that those figures were messengers waiting for my willingness to listen. I went to my journal, picked up a pen, and began listening.

Four days after the meeting, I awakened to the memory of being a shipping magnate in England. I was in a state of despair because one of my sea captains was always taking enormous risks with my cargoes. I remembered a memory of another lifetime when the same sea captain had left me standing on the docks. This particular scenario was being repeated—almost like a do-over, and I realized he was being given a chance for new choices.

The sea captain was our group's teacher in this lifetime. This new information about the wizard had me pulling other puzzle pieces together. I began connecting several students from that original classroom to some important male figures in my current lifetime. I sat for meditation, asking my guides to help me understand the meaning of each relationship. My guides showed me that one of my young students had betrayed me and stabbed me in the heart.

When I heard those words, I felt myself falling to the floor with the fabric of my robes collapsing around me. My guides told me that this was why I had been told to stay away from him in this lifetime. He was still jealous and lacked unconditional integrity.

My favorite student was a blond, green-eyed young man who was fit, handsome, and gifted. He was shy about his skills, especially after recognizing how easily he could complete any of the lessons I presented to him. The work he was able to do so easily seemed to become a huge burden, and he would never practice outside of the classroom. He was the same way in this lifetime. For those of us who can see the colors and energies around a person, there would be a beautiful indigo light when he worked on people that descended from God/Source directed by his hands to the client on his table.

With the realization that I was meeting some of these students in this lifetime, I began watching for them. I found three of them right away. They were all fifteen to seventeen years younger than I was, and I soon began calling them my forty-something friends. Over the next few years, another three or four of them came into my life. One of them must have been another favorite student. As soon as I met him, there was a warm feeling. He seemed to feel how much I liked him; during one of his classes, he looked me in the eye and stated with an equally warm feeling that he knew how much I liked him. I just smiled because I did like him in the way a teacher likes to see a student excel.

I never did tell any of these men about our past lives together, but as I met each one, I learned to more easily recognize what needed reconciling in this lifetime.

Final Comments

I still have my talks with the Universe, asking for help in discovering what was blocking my movement forward. When I finished this book and sent the manuscript to the publisher the first time, I felt completely overwhelmed. I stared at a copy of the manuscript for hours. I missed a painting class. I turned off the computer. I felt that there should have been some kind of jumping up and down kind of joy in feeling finished. While I was happy to be finished, there was now a void that I can only describe as the emptiness felt after the rush of a carnival ride or the near miss of a serious accident. When I first moved to Houston, I had a feeling that I was about to jump from the edge of a cliff. I had already considered that move an adventure, but it had turned into the beginning of some greater adventure that involved my getting reacquainted with my inner self. That scary feeling eventually disintegrated when I found—and continued—my personal and spiritual work.

There has also been an unexpected healing, while working on this manuscript. An idea for my next book started twisting around in my head. There was one lengthy, detailed event in my early teens that surfaced while taking some energy classes. The information could fill an entire book by itself, but I refused to write down anything until *Paint to Remember* was finished.

As soon as I felt finished with the first draft of the manuscript, I had no desire to write about that new idea. This loss of desire reminded me of personal healing sessions and the healing process that often followed. The release of personal emotional issues that were directly related to the barriers in my life often resulted in a significant, long-lasting detachment from the related emotions. That detachment often meant that the memory dissolved to the point of having to focus on trying to remember what had caused the problem in the first place.

The first time this happened to me, I was totally amazed. There was no point in trying to remember because—once you find yourself free of that invisible brick wall—there is no reason or desire to return to it. Finishing the manuscript acted like the processing time after a healing session and had inadvertently created a detachment from the childhood memories that were only posing as an idea for the next book. In reality, those childhood memories were just looking for a way to be released.

To fill that void, I turned my attention to painting. I began looking at the art supplies that I had been collecting since high school, de-cluttered a bit, and tossed out a few items that had to have been thirty years old. This made room for a new collection of supplies that have become my daily working tools.

This book would not have happened if I hadn't been reunited with Ceci and the two other guides who came to me while I wrote in my journals. Henry was one of my protectors. He was with me in many, many lifetimes and seemed to always have some version of the same name. The third guide was really an angel who often cheered me on while I worked. I never saw his face, but I did see his heavy cotton tunic swing back and forth as he did a happy dance for one of my accomplishments.

Rainbow Rain Meditation

Find a quiet place and sit or lie down in a comfortable position.

Start with a deep breath and remember the brightest and most colorful rainbow that you have ever seen. Remember your favorite colors and remember how good you felt for having had a chance to enjoy it. As you watch it a fluffiness begins to form around the edges of each color. Continue watching as each color separates from the others to become a cloud.

Pause and take another deep breath as the clouds begin shuffling around the space above you. Notice that the color in each of the clouds begins to brighten and glimmer. The clouds appear to become bigger as if full of moisture. You begin to feel the raindrops fall gently onto your body.

Take a few moments to enjoy this shower of color, breathing gently as the raindrops wash away anything that is not in your highest good.

The clouds begin shuffling around again creating a mixture of all colors falling all over your body, washing away remnants of any stress and pain. Breathe in the healing moisture of the colors. The colors begin to fade and all the clouds form one large sparkling white cloud. This cloud gently dissolves to reveal a clear blue sky.

Take a few deep breathes, slowly begin to move your body around and open your eyes.

My Favorite Books

Chinese Qigong Massage, Yang Jwing-Ming, 1994.

The Energy and Geometry of Sacred Sites, Tyberonn, 2007 (available at earth-keeper.com).

Energy Healing: A Pathway to Inner Growth, Jim Gilkeson, 1999.

Feelings Buried Alive Never Die, Karol K. Truman, 1991.

The Force, Stuart Wilde, 1995.

Heal Your Body: The Mental Causes for Physical Illness Louise Hay, 1985.

Life Energy: Using the Meridians to Unlock the Hidden Power of Your Emotions. John Diamond, 1998.

Messages from the Body: Their Psychological Meaning, Michael J. Lincoln, 2006.

The Soul's Remembrance, Roy Mills, 1999.

Touch for Health: A Practical Guide to Natural Health with Acupressure Touch, John Thie and Matthew Thie, 2005.

Writing down the Bones, Natalie Goldberg, 1986.

Walking Between the Worlds: The Science of Compassion, Gregg Braden, 1997.

About the Author

Katherine lives in Springfield, Missouri with her dog, Ruby Rose. After twenty-six years in the corporate world, she changed careers to offer and teach massage therapy. Her goal was to help others learn how to heal themselves through releasing the emotional attachments to trauma in this and other lifetimes. She often sees the lingering emotion of a traumatic event in a person's body and can help the willing client release the cause of some issue in their life—most times without the client having to remember the event. Katherine currently devotes most of her time to writing and painting.

CPSIA information can be obtained at www.ICGtesting.com
Printed in the USA
LVOW110806131012

302671LV00002B/2/P